PILOTS
TO
NEW YORK

NC6 337

ALEXANDER
EAGLEROCK

For Dylan, Dean, and Lauren—
spread your wings and fly! Love you always!
—L.J.

For Emelia and Hallie: the sky's the limit. Love you!
—S.B.

For my dear friend Patti Lee Gauch
—F.C.

Text copyright © 2021 by Louisa Jaggar
Jacket art and interior illustrations copyright © 2021 by Floyd Cooper
All rights reserved. Published in the United States by Crown Books for Young Readers, an imprint of Random
House Children's Books, a division of Penguin Random House LLC, New York.
Crown and the colophon are registered trademarks of Penguin Random House LLC.

Visit us on the Web! rhcbooks.com
Educators and librarians, for a variety of teaching tools, visit us at RHTeachersLibrarians.com

Library of Congress Cataloging-in-Publication Data
Names: Jaggar, Louisa, author. | Becker, Shari, author. | Cooper, Floyd, illustrator.
Title: Sprouting wings: the flying hobos: the true story of James Herman Banning, the first
African American pilot to fly across the United States / Louisa Jaggar, Shari Becker,
illustrations by Floyd Cooper.
Description: First edition. | New York: Crown Books for Young Readers, [2021] | Includes bibliographical
references. | Audience: Ages 5–7. | Audience: Grades K–1. | Summary: "The true story of James Herman
Banning, the first African American pilot to fly across the United States"—Provided by publisher.
Identifiers: LCCN 2019057115 (print) | LCCN 2019057116 (ebook)
ISBN 978-1-9848-4762-1 (hardback) | ISBN 978-1-9848-4763-8 (library binding)
ISBN 978-1-9848-4765-2 (trade paperback) | ISBN 978-1-9848-4764-5 (ebook)
Subjects: LCSH: Banning, James Herman—Juvenile literature. | African American air pilots—
Biography—Juvenile literature. | Cross-country flying—United States—Juvenile literature.
Classification: LCC TL540.B354 J34 2021 (print) | LCC TL540.B354 (ebook)
DDC 629.13092 [B]—dc23

The text of this book is set in Archer Medium.
The illustrations in this book were created using oil paint on board.
Book design by Martha Rago

MANUFACTURED IN CHINA
10 9 8 7 6 5 4 3 2 1
First Edition

Random House Children's Books supports the First Amendment
and celebrates the right to read.

Louisa Jaggar & Shari Becker

SPROUTING WINGS

The True Story of James Herman Banning,
the First African American Pilot
to Fly Across the United States

Illustrated by **Floyd Cooper**

Crown Books for Young Readers ♔ New York

FIVE-YEAR-OLD JAMES HERMAN BANNING tore across the red dirt fields of his family's farm, clutching the string of his homemade kite. He loved the way the wind carried leaves and birds and scraps of paper on its back. And now it was carrying his third kite. The first had tumbled, then crashed. The second had fluttered and fallen, breaking on the ground—but his third kite took off! James looked up at the speck of paper on its cross of sticks and watched its cloth tail flap against the deep blue of Canton, Oklahoma's sky.

"One day," he said, "I'm goin' to build a kite big enough to ride on."

In early October 1905, James's father decided it was time to go to town. Going-to-town days meant crackers, peppermint sticks, and pieces of licorice.

Today, though, James could tell something was different. Men and women, girls and boys were talking loudly, waving their hands, clutching their newspapers. "A flying machine!" he heard someone call.

A flying machine? On the front page of *The Oklahoman*, James read that the Wright Brothers flew their airplane at Kitty Hawk, North Carolina, for sixteen and a half minutes in the air.

James didn't need a big kite to touch the sky.

He needed a flying machine.

EXCELSIOR
LIBRARY

Six years later, still no flying machines flew over the Banning homestead, but James didn't stop wondering how those mechanical birds stayed up in the air. Luckily, twice a year, Ma and Pa took them all to Guthrie, eighty-two miles away, to the Excelsior Library—the first Black library in all of Oklahoma. Here, in a ramshackle Victorian filled with other people's thrown-away books, he found information about flying machines and flight. About lift, force, and drag. About real birdmen taking them into the sky. One newspaper headline said that Charles Walsh, a birdman, was bringing his plane to the local fair in Thomas on November 10, 1911. Thomas was only eight miles away.

On November 10, the fairground was packed. Walsh's pusher plane swooped low and buzzed the crowd. Then, *rat-a-tat-tat*, the plane landed. Walsh climbed out to whoops and hollers.

All James could see was the plane. His hands itched to touch the metal bird. James dashed to the plane and climbed through the spiderweb of wires and cords. Then he sat in the kitchen chair nailed to the floor. He closed his eyes and flew.

"A boy! In the plane!" people shouted—but James didn't hear them. He didn't turn to see Walsh running up to the pusher.

"Hey, get away from there!" Walsh yelled.

James scrambled out of the plane and ran, but he could still smell the oil and gas, feel the controls in his hand.

He was still flying.

On June 28, 1914, the Great War broke out in Europe.
Planes covered the fronts of newspapers and magazines: Bristol Type 22s, Fokker Eindeckers, and Sopwith Camels. At the Gem Theater, for five cents or an egg—yes, a chicken egg—James watched newsreels with awe as fighter planes swooped through the air.

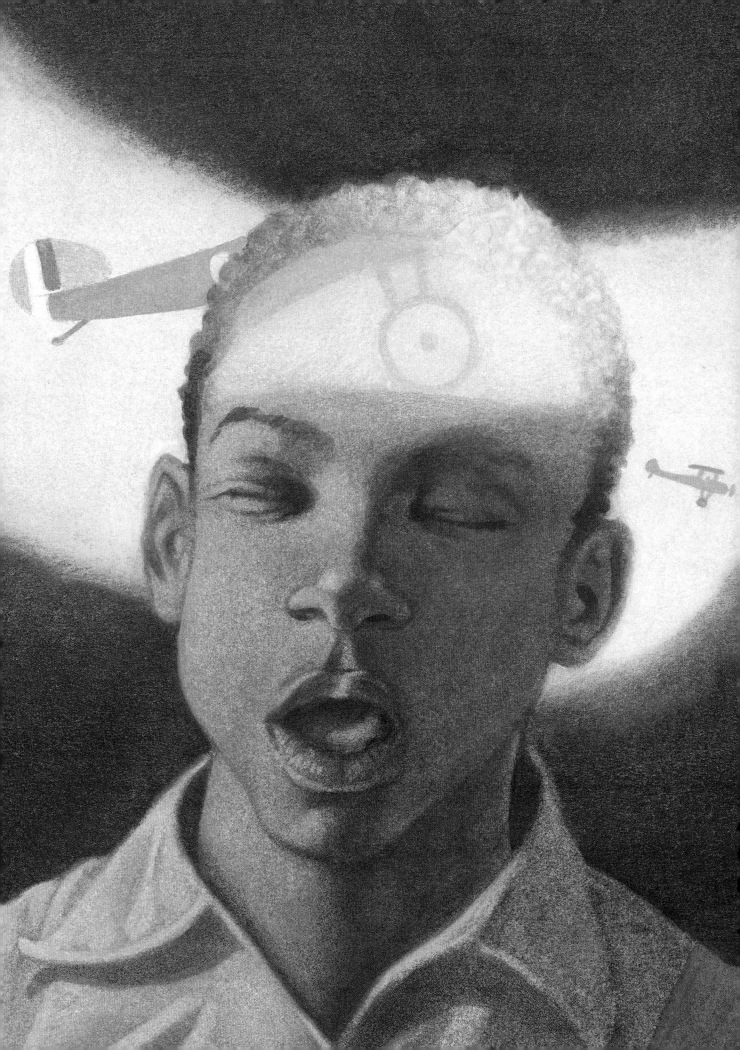

When James graduated from Faver High School, he did what none of his friends or family had ever done before: he applied to college. He was one of only seven Black students accepted into Iowa State that year. Though his grades were good, money was so tight he could only go for one year. Even so, he held on to his dream of becoming a birdman.

When Banning was twenty-one, he opened his own business in Ames, Iowa: Banning Auto Company. He fixed motorcycles and automobiles and farm equipment, all the while looking for someone who would teach him to fly. There were birdmen and birdwomen in Iowa, designing aeroplanes, building airfields, and starting flight schools, but no one would teach Banning, a Black man.

Then one day a man pushed a broken motorcycle into Banning's shop. Banning noticed the military aviator wings on the man's leather jacket. His name was Lieutenant Raymond Fisher, and he was a pilot! He asked Fisher if he would teach him to fly.

Lieutenant Fisher didn't care that Banning was Black. He only cared that Banning wanted to fly.

This time the answer was yes.

Banning met Fisher at dawn, and both men climbed into Fisher's Curtiss Jenny biplane.

Banning gently pushed the throttle full forward. The engine roared as the plane hopscotched down the runway. The Jenny's nose lifted and caught the wind under her wings. Banning could hear the roar and smell the oil and taste the wind.

A year later, it was time for him to solo! But on
April 12, 1926, when Banning arrived at Fisher's field,
he found a mangled metal bird. Fisher's Jenny had
crashed, and Fisher had died that very morning.
Banning was heartbroken. He'd lost his friend and
the one person helping him take to the skies.

Banning still needed solo hours to earn his pilot's license, but no one would lend him an aeroplane, so he decided to build his own. He bought a spare engine at an auction, purchased a Jenny fuselage, and scavenged wires, cords, and automobile parts. He put the pieces together in a nearby cow pasture. With the help of five friends, Banning built his first plane.

But was it even safe to fly? Banning wasn't sure. Every day he climbed into his plane, started the motor, partially opened the throttle, and slowly, slowly drove it in circles on the ground. This became the town joke: Banning and his "ground plane."

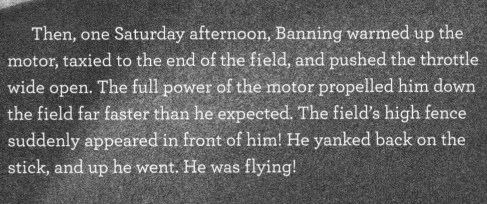

Then, one Saturday afternoon, Banning warmed up the motor, taxied to the end of the field, and pushed the throttle wide open. The full power of the motor propelled him down the field far faster than he expected. The field's high fence suddenly appeared in front of him! He yanked back on the stick, and up he went. He was flying!

"I have sprouted wings!" James Herman Banning shouted to the clouds.

Banning received his pilot's license, number 1324. But he still wanted more. He wanted to learn to barnstorm: to loop-the-loop, to barrel roll, and to make a dead-stick landing. His first loops didn't loop and his rolls didn't roll, but Banning didn't give up. Soon he was circling the sky and rolling across the clouds. He had taught himself to barnstorm!

In California, 1,719 miles away, a man named William Powell dreamed that freedom in the air would one day lead to freedom on the ground. He wanted to open a flight school for Black men and women.

So Powell opened the Bessie Coleman Aero Club and went looking for a Black pilot.

He sent a letter to the Negro Associated Press, and it appeared in the *California Eagle*, the *New York Amsterdam News*, the *Pittsburgh Courier*, and the *Chicago Defender*.

It also appeared in the *Iowa Bystander* in November 1929. As soon as Banning read Powell's letter, he knew he was the pilot Powell needed. He began packing that very day and moved to Los Angeles. Powell hired Banning on the spot as chief pilot.

In the next three years, Banning taught air-minded Black men and women to fly and to perform aerobatic stunts. On September 7, 1931, Powell and Banning put on the first all-Black air show.

In 1932, Banning left the aero club to follow a new dream: he wanted to be the first Black man to fly from Los Angeles to New York. All he needed was a plane. His friend Arthur Dennis had a dilapidated Eaglerock with a fourteen-year-old engine. It needed a lot of work.

Thomas Cox Allen, a local aeroplane mechanic, didn't have a pilot's license, but he knew how to make engines, even old engines, roar. He also had 200 dollars.

Banning and Allen didn't get along well, but they shared the hope of being the first Black men to fly cross-country. They fixed the Eaglerock, replacing pistons, spark plugs, and the overhead action valve. When they were done, they had only twenty-five dollars left.

Banning and Allen scoured a map and looked for towns and cities where they knew people, where people had skin the color of theirs. They charted a route through towns and cities where it would be safe for them to land.

At every stop, family, friends, townspeople, city folk, church congregations—anyone, everyone who helped them with a meal, a place to sleep, or gas money—would get to sign their names on the Gold Book: the wings of the Eaglerock.

"Gee," said Allen. "We'll be just like hobos, begging our way."

"Fine," said Banning. "That gives me an idea."

"We'll call ourselves
the Flying Hobos."

On September 19, 1932, Banning and Allen took off from Dycer Airport in Los Angeles.

They flew from Alhambra to Riverside, California. From Yuma to Tucson, Arizona. Everywhere they went, people helped however they could: providing money, meals, transportation, lodging, gas, oil, repairs, and sometimes even spare plane parts.

But in Lordsburg, New Mexico, where the copper mines were empty and no one had any money, the Eaglerock ran out of gas. Allen sold his fancy suit, his only suit, to a Mr. R. C. Hightower for ten dollars, just enough money to get them to El Paso, Texas.

Banning and Allen flew on. Nineteen names were written on the Gold Book. Nineteen friends flying along with them. They flew from Wink to Midland, then on to Wichita Falls, Texas. But as they flew over the Guadalupe Mountains, they ran into fog so heavy they couldn't see their wingtips.

"We lucked through," said Banning when they came out of the fog.

They continued on to El Reno, Oklahoma, where Banning's brother Archibald lived.

As they headed to Oklahoma City, thirty names were written on the Gold Book—thirty friends flying with them. They flew from Tulsa to Miami, Oklahoma. Then to Carthage, Missouri. At a pit stop in St. Louis, the tired bird's engine gave out again. A local mechanic school rebuilt it as a class project. In Terre Haute, Indiana, they fixed a broken push rod. In Columbus, Ohio, the people of the Second Baptist Church gave them five dollars.

Every stop brought them closer to New York, but they still had over 500 miles to go. As they approached Cambridge, Ohio, the Eaglerock's engine sputtered. The plane dropped. The engine rattled, then died.

There was a haystack on one side of them
and a barn on the other. Banning flew sideways
between the two, then righted the plane, pulling the
stick all the way back. As the wheels hit the ground,
the plane bounced like a jackrabbit. Banning had
made a perfect dead-stick landing.

The townspeople came running. Many had
never seen an aeroplane. None had ever seen a
Black man fly.

"The steel in our motor is so old, it's crystallized.
Two rocker arms went out," Banning said.

With the help of the townspeople, black and white, Banning and Allen got the Eaglerock back in the air. Banning thanked the people with a loop and a barrel roll. The Flying Hobos flew on with sixty-eight names inscribed on the Gold Book: sixty-eight friends flying with them.

The Eaglerock's engine died again as they landed in Pittsburgh, Pennsylvania, home to the *Pittsburgh Courier*. Banning had been writing about the flight for the newspaper: "Coast–to–Coast, Via the Aerial Highways." The editor, Mr. Robert Lee Vann, said he would pay to fix the Eaglerock if they tossed 150,000 vote-for-Roosevelt campaign flyers out of the plane. Banning agreed. They headed to York, then to Philadelphia. Then on to West Trenton, New Jersey, where they spent the night.

Now seventy-two names were written on the Gold Book.

"There is not one inch of space on our old Eaglerock that is not written on," said Banning.

On October 9, 1932, at 9:15 in the morning, Banning and Allen gassed up the Eaglerock. They checked the engine and the oil. Allen hand-propped the propeller. Banning took off. Soon they were in New York.

Banning looped around Lady Liberty once to let her know they'd made it.

Banning and Allen landed in Valley Stream, New York, after traveling for twenty-one days with the help of twenty-four communities. They had used 410 gallons of gas and spent 150 dollars to fly 3,300 miles to the other side of the country.

That night they celebrated with the biggest stars in Harlem:
Cab Calloway, Mrs. Bill "Bojangles" Robinson, and Louis Armstrong.
After years of dreaming, Banning and Allen were stars, too.

A Note from Louisa Jaggar

AROUND THE TIME researcher Pat Smith stumbled upon a small newspaper article written about James Herman Banning's transcontinental flight, I welcomed my first grandson, Dylan, into the world. Dylan is African American, and Banning's incredible story is a story I wanted him to know. Yet there was very little information available. The more Pat and I learned, the more fascinated we became. We spent seven years digging up every scrap of information we could.

We sought primary sources that detailed Banning's life: journals, newspaper articles, first-person interviews, oral histories, records, and documents.

We began our search by interviewing Banning's great-nephew Philip Hart, who shared photographs and stories about the family. Pat, who lived in Oklahoma, then went searching through museum attics. At the bottom of a beaten-up cardboard box, she discovered Thomas Cox Allen's original unpublished manuscript detailing the flight. She couldn't believe what she'd found! Not only did Allen describe the flight, but he also wrote down the name of every person who'd signed the Gold Book, what they donated, and what state they were from. We shared our exciting research with Lonnie Bunch, the director of the Smithsonian's National Museum of African American History and Culture.

We read William Powell's memoir, *Black Aviator*, in which Powell talked about Banning and Allen in detail. Though mainstream papers did not cover Banning and Allen's heroic flight, over two hundred African American newspapers reported on their great adventure—including Banning's own account in a series of articles published by the *Pittsburgh Courier*. We found the articles through sources such as ProQuest on the internet and on microfiche in public libraries, in the Library of Congress, and in universities. We are still discovering more.

These primary documents allowed me to find quotes from Banning and Allen, and these direct quotes are sprinkled throughout this book.

It is a great tragedy that prejudice ultimately cost Banning his life. He was

scheduled to fly a number of stunts in an Airtech air show in San Diego, but the chief flight instructor, Arnet Spear, refused to allow Banning to fly in one of his planes. An unlicensed white naval mechanic, Albert Burghardt, offered Banning the use of Burghardt's friend's plane. The catch? Burghardt wanted to perform a stunt at the air show and wanted Banning to fly with him. Banning agreed to go as his passenger. The mechanic attempted a loop but stalled the plane, and the plane spun to the ground in front of two thousand horrified spectators. Banning died that day, February 5, 1933.

Quotation Sources

"One day . . . I'm goin' to build a kite big enough to ride on." and "Hey, get away from there!": Levette, Harry. "J. Herman Banning Mourned 'Ace of the Air,' Showed Early Interest in Flying." *New Journal and Guide* (an African American newspaper), March 11, 1933.

"On the front page of *The Oklahoman*, James read that the Wright Brothers flew their airplane at Kitty Hawk, North Carolina, for sixteen and a half minutes in the air.": "Air Navigated in Beautiful Tests." *The Oklahoman*, July 18, 1909. Paraphrased in text.

"Will you teach me to fly?": Hart, Philip, interview. Paraphrased in text.

"This became the town joke: Banning and his ground plane." and "I have sprouted wings!": Banning, James Herman. "Pilot's Biggest Thrill Is First Time He Gets a Chance to Fly Solo." *The Pittsburgh Courier* (an African American newspaper), December 17, 1932.

"Gee . . . We'll be just like hobos, begging our way." and "Fine . . . That gives me an idea. We'll call ourselves the Flying Hobos.": Powell, William J. *Black Aviator, The Story of William J. Powell* (p. 114).

"We lucked through . . . The steel in our motor is so old, it's crystallized. Two rocker arms went out.": "Harlem Honors Coast-to-Coast Negro Flyers. First of Race to Cross Continent by Air Took Two Weeks to Make Trip." *New York Herald Tribune*, October 9, 1932.

"There is not one inch of space on our old Eaglerock that is not written on.": Gardner, Chappy. "2 Aviators End Flight Across U.S." *Atlanta Daily World* (an African American newspaper), October 13, 1932.

Newspaper Articles by James Herman Banning

"Coast-to-Coast, Via the Aerial Highways" (series of four articles detailing Banning's flight). *The Pittsburgh Courier* (an African American newspaper), October 22, 1932; October 29, 1932; November 5, 1932; November 12, 1932.

"I Am a Fugitive—from Injustice—Says Writer About Negro." *The Pittsburgh Courier,* December 31, 1932.

"The Negro and the Airplane." *The Pittsburgh Courier,* November 26, 1932.

Interviews

Allen, Thomas Cox, interviewed by Pen Allen Woods, February 2, 1978.

Allen, Thomas Cox, interviewed by unknown, at Oklahoma Historical Society at the Oklahoma Aerospace Museum, 1987.

Bunch, Lonnie G. (secretary of the Smithsonian Institution and founding director of Smithsonian Institution's National Museum of African American History and Culture), in discussion with the authors, October 10, 2017, and May 1, 2018.

Hardesty, Von (curator of the Smithsonian's *Black Wings* exhibit at the Smithsonian Institution's Air and Space Museum), in discussion with the authors, 2010–2016.

Hart, Philip (James Herman Banning's great-nephew), in discussion with the authors, January 9, 2009.

Documents

Banning family (including James Herman Banning). Dewey County Census. 1900, 1910, 1920.

Banning, James Herman. Iowa State College African American Student Directory. 226½ Main Street—Winter 1921. Roommates: Atwood, Rufus (1920–1923), Bibb, Cornelius C. (1920–1921), Patterson, Frederick D. (1920–1923), Smith, Clarence S. (1920–1922).

Banning, James Herman. Iowa State College Fall 1920 Entrance Card. August 20, 1920.

Banning, Riley W. (James Herman Banning's father). Oklahoma Homestead Deed (signed by President Theodore Roosevelt). December 31, 1903.

For Further Reading

Allen, Thomas Cox. Unpublished manuscript detailing the transcontinental flight, Oklahoma History Center, Oklahoma City.

Hardesty, Von. *Black Wings: Courageous Stories of African Americans in Aviation and Space History.* Washington, DC: Smithsonian Institution Press, 2008.

Powell, William J. *Black Aviator, The Story of William J. Powell.* Washington, DC: Smithsonian Institution Press, 1994. Originally published in 1934.

For a complete list of sources, visit jhbanning.com.

To the one-day leaders growing up
in Baltimore, Maryland, today
—CBW

To my parents, who immigrated forty-two
years ago to this land of opportunity
—CH

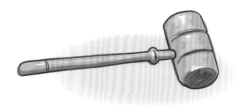

 little bee books

New York, NY
Text copyright © 2021 by Carole Boston Weatherford
Illustrations copyright © 2021 by Chris Hsu
All rights reserved, including the right of reproduction
in whole or in part in any form.
For information about special discounts on bulk purchases,
please contact Little Bee Books at sales@littlebeebooks.com.
Manufactured in China   RRD 0521
First Edition
2 4 6 8 10 9 7 5 3 1
ISBN 978-1-4998-1189-6
littlebeebooks.com

MADAM SPEAKER
NANCY PELOSI CALLS THE HOUSE TO ORDER

by Carole Boston Weatherford   illustrated by Chris Hsu

little bee books

Nancy D'Alesandro had a hand in politics from an early age,
stuffing envelopes, handing out leaflets,
and waving from a convertible as her father spoke
through a bullhorn during his political campaigns.
When he was sworn in as mayor, she held the Bible.

"I was raised in a large family that was devoutly Catholic, deeply patriotic, proud of our Italian American heritage, and staunchly Democratic."

Nancy placed her hand over her heart each day
to pledge allegiance to the flag, and her parents
taught her to always lend a helping hand.
She manned her father's home office,
dutifully noting citizens' needs and concerns.
She and her five brothers looked up
to the past presidents whose portraits hung in their home.
And they never looked down on those who needed a hand up.

"My parents taught us that public service was a noble calling, and that we had a responsibility to help those in need."

As a teenager, Nancy snapped her fingers to rock 'n' roll and seldom held a date's hand. How could she? Her parents always had one of her five big brothers chaperone. At a Catholic all-girls college prep school, she grasped the leadership lessons the nuns handed down.

At Trinity College in Washington, DC, Nancy pored over
political science textbooks and typed term papers.
She gained firsthand experience interning for elected officials.
She was thrilled to meet then Senator,
and later President, John F. Kennedy.
At JFK's inauguration, her hands joined the chorus
of applause for his stirring speech.
Ask not what your country can do for you—
ask what you can do for your country.

When Paul Pelosi, a student at nearby Georgetown University, asked for Nancy's hand in marriage, she said, "Yes." Within six years, the couple had five children and had moved from DC to New York to San Francisco. Nancy's hands were full! She enlisted her children to fold clothes, pack lunches, and set and clear the table. Just as her father had done during her childhood, she made sure that all hands were on deck.

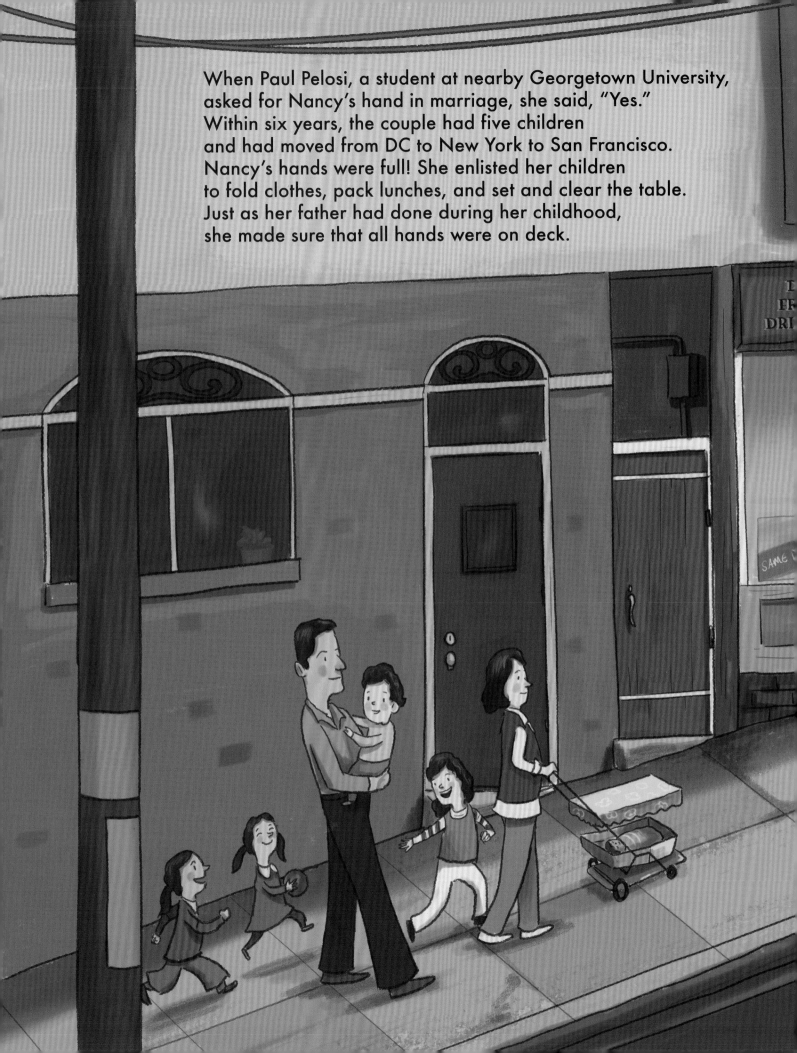

"What took me from the kitchen to Congress
was knowing that one in five children in America lives in poverty. . . .
America must be the light of the world."

When Pelosi raised her right hand to take her oath
as a congresswoman representing San Francisco,
her father—once a congressman himself—
proudly looked on from his wheelchair.

"In 1987, Congress was still pretty much a men's club.
I didn't come to Congress to change the attitudes of men.
I came to change the policies of our country."

Pelosi's nimble fingers joined those of her children in sewing a square for the AIDS Memorial Quilt that, thanks to her efforts, blanketed the National Mall. She also penned laws to protect gay rights.

Pelosi gained so much respect among her congressional peers
that she was elected House Minority Leader in 2003
and four years later, Speaker of the House—
the first woman to be second in line to the presidency.

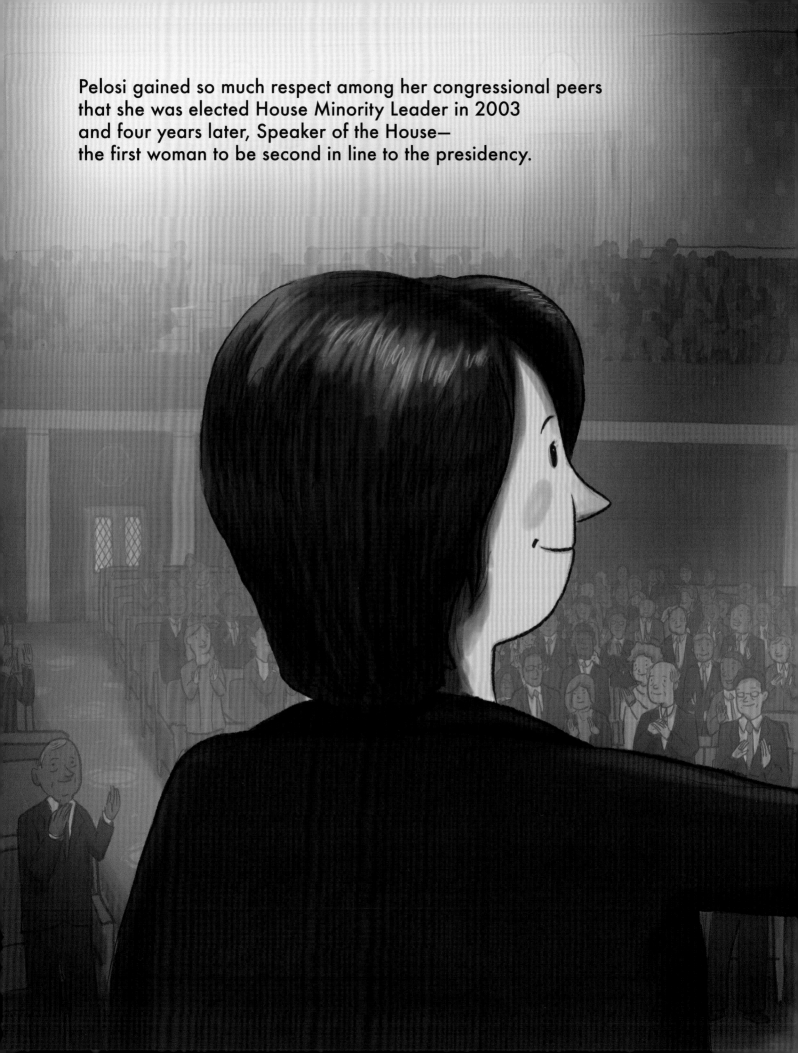

After Pelosi's party was handed a defeat in the midterm election,
Pelosi became Minority Leader again in 2011.
But she kept working on the causes closest to her heart.
In 2018, she set a House record, speaking for over eight hours
to protect "Dreamers," the children of undocumented immigrants.

"We have a responsibility to find our common ground.
But when we can't find our common ground,
we must stand our ground."

The elder stateswoman punctuates her speech
with elegant yet forceful hand gestures,
and dares to point out injustice whenever she sees it,
maintaining the upper hand with a mix
of strength, wisdom, and strategy.

"Anybody who's ever dealt with me
knows not to mess with me."

With faith guiding her public service, Pelosi prays for presidents, popes, and ordinary people alike. She shapes emerging leaders by sheer example.

"It's about having faith in yourself, having faith in God, having faith in our country, having faith in the future."

The same hands that have held sway over her party combed her granddaughter's hair just before the two of them walked into the House Chamber in 2018 as history prepared to repeat itself.

Pelosi beckoned children to join her on the podium
while she took the oath as Speaker for the second time.

"I call the House to order on behalf
of all of America's children."

Nancy Pelosi gripped the handle and sounded the gavel.

CLACK!

And with that,
Madam Speaker had spoken.

Nancy Pelosi Biography

March 26, 1940
Nancy Patricia D'Alesandro is born into a Roman Catholic and politically active family in Baltimore, Maryland.

1958
Graduates from the Institute of Notre Dame, a Catholic high school for girls.

1962
Graduates from Trinity College in Washington, DC, with a bachelor of arts in political science.

1963
Marries Paul Pelosi, and together, they raise five children: Nancy, Christine, Jacqueline, Paul Jr., and Alexandra.

1969
Pelosi family moves to San Francisco, California.

1976–1996
Serves as California representative to the Democratic National Committee.

1981–1983
Chairs the California Democratic Party.

1987
Like her father, a former congressman and mayor of Baltimore, and her brother, also a former Baltimore mayor, she enters electoral politics, winning a special election for California's 5th (now 12th) Congressional seat.

Serves on the House Appropriations Committee, Permanent Select Committee on Intelligence, and the House Baltic Caucus.

2001
Elected House Minority Whip, second-in-command to the Minority Leader and the first woman elected to the position.

2003–2007
Becomes highest-ranking woman in Congressional history upon election as House Minority Leader.

2007–2011
Another first—elected the 52nd Speaker of the House, second in the presidential line of succession to the Vice President.

2010
Wins House and Senate passage of the Affordable Care Act (ACA), expanding health care access to millions of Americans.

2011–2019
Becomes Minority Leader of the House a second time after Republicans gain a majority in Congress.

February 7, 2018

Delivers an eight-hour speech (in four-inch heels) on the House floor for legislation affecting young children of undocumented people brought to the United States (Dreamers).

2019

Begins her 17th term in Congress.

After Democrats regain the majority, she is re-elected Speaker of the House, the first former speaker to win re-election to the post since Sam Rayburn in 1955.

Cancels the annual State of the Union address (which would be rescheduled) in protest over Administration policies.

Issues the first House rebuke of a sitting president in more than 100 years over President Trump's comments on Democratic female congresswomen.

Calls for a vote on two articles of impeachment for presidential "abuse of power" and "obstruction of Congress" that are passed by the House, but defeated by the Senate.

2020

In an act of defiance, publicly shreds her copy of the State of the Union address immediately following its conclusion.

Bibliography

Abel, Allen. (2019, February 5). The Nancy walking all over Trump. Retrieved from macleans.ca/politics/washington/the-nancy-walking-all-over-trump/

Brewington, Kelly. (2006, November 9). "Bursting with pride" in Little Italy. Retrieved from baltimoresun.com/bal-littleitaly110906-story.html

Davies, Frank. (2006, October 7). Family dynasty may boost Pelosi to head of House. Retrieved eastbaytimes.com/2006/10/07/family-dynasty-may-boost-pelosi-to-head-of-house-2/

Duke, Lynne. (2006, November 10). Pride of Baltimore Nancy Pelosi Learned Her Politics at the Elbow of Her Father the Mayor. Retrieved from washingtonpost.com/archive/lifestyle/2006/11/10/pride-of-baltimore-span-classbankheadnancy-pelosi-learned-her-politics-at-the-elbow-of-her-father-the-mayorspan/3325ffd8-f733-49fa-a920-0f259d07ad43/

Feuerherd, Joe. (2003, January 24). Roots in faith, family and party guide Pelosi's move to power. Retrieved from natcath.org/NCR_Online/archives/012403/012403a.htm

Marbella, Jean. (2010, December 18). Giving up the gavel, Pelosi looks to the future. Retrieved from baltimoresun.com/maryland/bs-xpm-2010-12-18-bs-md-nancy-pelosi-20101218-story.html

McCarthy, Ellen. (2019, February 12). Makes going to work look easy: Decades before she was House speaker, Nancy Pelosi had an even harder job. Retrieved from washingtonpost.com/lifestyle/style/makes-going-to-work-look-easy-how-being-a-full-time-mom-prepared-nancy-pelosi-for-this-moment/2019/02/12/416cd85e-28bc-11e9-984d-9b8fba003e81_story.html

Neuman, Johanna. (2002, November 11). Nancy Pelosi on Brink of Breaking a Barrier for Women. Retrieved from dailypress.com/news/dp-xpm-20021111-2002-11-11-0211110075-story.html

Pelosi, Nancy. (2007, January 4). Pelosi Calls for a New America, Built on the Values that Made Our Country Great. Retrieved from speaker.gov/newsroom/pelosi-calls-new-america-built-values-made-country-great

Pelosi, Nancy. (2018, May 20). Pelosi Commencement Address at Mount Holyoke College. Retrieved from speaker.gov/newsroom/52018

School Sisters of Notre Dame, Atlantic-Midwest Province. (Undated). How Nancy Pelosi's Baltimore Catholic Roots Shaped Her. Retrieved from atlanticmidwest.org/posts/how-nancy-pelosis-baltimore-catholic-roots-shaped-her